SECRETS TO LIVE WITH GRATITUDE

CULTIVATING AN ATTITUDE OF APPRECIATION

DR. JAGADEESH PILLAI

Made with ♥ on the Notion Press Platform
www.notionpress.com

|| Dedicated to all wisdom seekers around the World ||

ॐ

Contents

Contents

Prayer

"Om Bhadram Karnebhih Shrunuyaama DevaahBhadram Pashyemaakshabhiryajatraah SthirairangaistushtuvaamsastanoobhihVyashema Devahitam YadaayuhSwasti Na Indro VridhashravaahSwasti Nah Pooshaa VishwavedaahSwasti Nastaarkshyo ArishtanemihSwasti No Brihaspatir DadhaatuOm Shantih, Shantih, Shantih"

The literal meaning of this mantra is: OM. O Gods! Let us hear auspicious words from our ears. O reverent Gods! Let us behold propitious visions from our eyes, let our organs and body be stable, healthy, and strong. Let us do that which is pleasing to the gods in the life span allotted to us. May Indra, inscribed in the scriptures, bring us fortune! May Pushan, the knower of the world, grant us prosperity! May Trakshya, who vanquishes enemies, bestow us with blessings! May Brihaspati bring us success!
OM Peace, Peace, Peace.

About The Author

Dr. Jagadeesh Pillai is a renowned Guinness World Record holder, writer, and researcher hailing from Varanasi, also known as the abode of Lord Shiva. With a Ph.D. in Vedic Science and a range of creative ideas and achievements, he is a true polymath. He is the author of more than 100 books including Research Publications. Although his roots can be traced back to Kerala, the people of Varanasi hold him in high regard and affectionately consider him one of their own.

In 1998, Dr. Pillai was offered a job at Banaras Hindu University, but he left the position after only two months to pursue greater goals in life. He believed that in order to study Indian scriptures and engage in other creative endeavours, he needed to retire from the daily grind of working solely for money at a young age.

He started an export business from scratch, using the knowledge he had gained from a previous job in the industry. His intelligence and unique approach to business led to great success in a short period of time, earning him more in just a decade and a half than he would have in a lifetime working in a government job. Upon the passing of Dr. APJ Abdul Kalam, Dr. Pillai decided to leave the business and dedicate himself to reading, studying, researching, and experimenting.

During his tenure in the export business, Dr. Pillai traveled to over 16 countries, gaining valuable insight and experiencing the world and life in detail.

Dr. Pillai has achieved four Guinness World Records in the following subjects:

"Script to Screen" - In this record, Dr. Pillai produced and directed an animation film within the shortest time possible, breaking the previous record set by Canadians. He has also received numerous national and international awards and recognitions for this achievement.

Longest Line of Postcards - For this record, Dr. Pillai created a line of 16,300 postcards on the occasion of the 163rd anniversary of Indian Postal Day. The event also included a questionnaire about the Indian flag.

Largest Poster Awareness Campaign - Dr. Pillai designed an awareness campaign on the subject of "Beti Bachao - Beti Padhao" (Save the Girl Child - Educate the Girl Child) to achieve this record.

Largest Envelope - In tribute to the Indian Prime Minister's "Make in India" initiative, Dr. Pillai created a 4000 square meter envelope using waste paper to achieve this record.

Attempted - **70000 Candles on a 210 kg Cake** - To celebrate the 70th Indian Independence Day, Dr. Pillai attempted to light 70,000 candles on a 210 kg cake, which was recorded in World Records India.

Attempted - **Documentary on Dhamek Stupa of Sarnath in 17 Languages** - Dr. Pillai attempted to create a documentary on the Dhamek Stupa of Sarnath, dubbing it in 17 different languages. The result of this attempt is currently awaiting confirmation from the Guinness World Records.

Dr. Pillai is skilled in teaching the Bhagavad Gita, a Hindu scripture, and is popular among young people. He has helped many young people improve their lives through his motivational teachings.

In addition to teaching, he has composed and sung numerous Sanskrit Bhajans and patriotic songs.

He has also written and directed several short films and documentaries for awareness campaigns, and has volunteered with the police in both UP and Kerala to spread awareness about various issues through videos and photography.

Incredibly, he has produced and directed over 100 documentaries about the city of Varanasi, all on his own.

He has also helped and guided more than 25 boys and girls to achieve world records through creative and innovative methods. He is a multifaceted person who uses his intellect and the blessings given to him by God to excel in various areas. He is both a teacher and a student, always learning and teaching, and is able to master any subject he comes across.

He is a selfless social activist and motivational speaker who has overcome struggles and failures to become a successful and enthusiastic individual with a rich life experience.

In addition to his work with the Bhagavad Gita, he is also an efficient Tarot card reader, Astro-Vastu consultant, and a talented singer and composer. He has sung the entire Ram Charita Manas and Bhagavad Gita in his own compositions, and has sung the phrase "Lokah Samastha Sukhino Bhavantu" in 50 different languages. He is currently working on a detailed and scientific study of Vedas, Upanishads, Puranas, and the Bhagavad Gita. He has also composed and sung the Hanuman Chalisa and Gayatri Mantra in 108 and 1008 different compositions, respectively.

Awards - Four Times Guinness World Records, Winner of Mahatma Gandhi Vishwa Shanti Puraskar, Mahatma Gandhi Global Peace Ambassador, Kashi Ratna Award, Dr. APJ Abdul Kalam Motivational Person of the Year 2017, Mother Teresa Award, Indira Gandhi Priyadarshini Award, Bharat Vikas Ratna Award, Udyog Ratna Award, Vigyan Prasar Award, Poorvanchal Ratn Samman.

PREFACE

In this book, "Secrets to Live with Gratitude: Cultivating an Attitude of Appreciation," readers will discover the power of cultivating an attitude of gratitude and appreciation in their lives. Through this book, readers will learn how to recognize and appreciate the beauty and abundance in their lives, and how to use this appreciation to create a more meaningful and fulfilling life.

This book is a guide to living with gratitude and appreciation, and it is filled with practical advice and inspiring stories. It will help readers to recognize the blessings in their lives, and to develop an attitude of gratitude and appreciation. It will also provide readers with the tools and strategies they need to cultivate an attitude of appreciation and to live a life of joy and contentment.

This book is a must-read for anyone who wants to live a life of gratitude and appreciation. It is a powerful reminder of the importance of recognizing and appreciating the beauty and abundance in our lives. It is a guide to living with gratitude and appreciation, and it will help readers to create a more meaningful and fulfilling life. So, if you are looking for a way to live with more gratitude and appreciation, this book is for you.

I

Understanding the Power of Gratitude and Appreciation

Gratitude and appreciation are two of the most powerful tools we can use to enhance our lives. These simple acts of acknowledging what we have, and expressing thanks for it, can have profound impacts on our happiness, well-being, and overall satisfaction with life.

At its core, gratitude is an acknowledgement of the good things we have in our lives. This can be anything from the big things, like having a roof over our heads and food to eat, to the smaller things, like a beautiful sunrise or a kind word from a friend.

Appreciation, on the other hand, is a deeper level of gratitude. It involves taking time to reflect on the good things in our lives, and actively focusing on and savoring these experiences. This can involve taking the time to really notice the beauty of nature, or to truly savor a delicious meal.

Both gratitude and appreciation have been shown to have powerful impacts on our well-being. Research has found that people who regularly practice gratitude and appreciation experience a range of benefits, including:

Increased happiness and life satisfaction:

When we focus on the good things in our lives, we are more likely to experience feelings of happiness and contentment.

Improved relationships:

Gratitude and appreciation can help to build and strengthen relationships, as we are more likely to focus on the positive aspects of our interactions with others.

Reduced stress and anxiety:

By focusing on the good things in our lives, we can reduce feelings of stress and anxiety, and increase feelings of calm and peace.

Improved physical health:

Gratitude and appreciation have been linked to better sleep, reduced symptoms of depression and anxiety, and improved immune function.

Increased resilience:

When we focus on what we are grateful for, we are more likely to be resilient in the face of challenges, and more likely to bounce back from setbacks.

So, what can you do to start cultivating an attitude of gratitude and appreciation in your own life? Here are a few tips:

Keep a gratitude journal:

Write down three things you are grateful for each day, no matter how small they may seem. This can help you to focus on the good things in your life, and to start seeing the world in a more positive light.

Practice mindfulness: Take time each day to focus on the present moment, and to really savor the experiences you are having. This can help you to increase feelings of gratitude and appreciation.

Express gratitude:

Take time to express your thanks to others, whether it be through a simple thank you note, or by expressing your gratitude in person.

Focus on the good:

When faced with challenges or setbacks, try to focus on the good things in your life, and on what you have to be grateful for.

By incorporating these practices into your daily life, you can start to cultivate an attitude of gratitude and appreciation, and experience the many benefits that come along with it. So, start today, and start living your best life!

Gratitude is the key to unlocking a life of joy and contentment; it is the secret to cultivating an attitude of appreciation and appreciation. By making the conscious decision to focus on the positive and be thankful, we can unlock a world of joy and contentment that will bring us a greater sense of fulfillment and satisfaction.

ᘓᘐ

II

Connecting to Gratitude and Appreciation in Daily Life

Gratitude and appreciation are powerful tools that can help us to lead happier, more fulfilling lives. However, it can be difficult to connect with these feelings on a daily basis, especially in the midst of our busy and often stressful lives. In this chapter, we will explore some simple strategies for incorporating gratitude and appreciation into your daily life, so that you can experience the benefits of this positive mindset.

Start the day with gratitude:

Begin each day by taking a moment to reflect on the things

you are grateful for. This can be as simple as making a mental list or writing down three things you are thankful for. By starting your day with gratitude, you will be setting a positive tone for the rest of the day.

Practice mindfulness:

Take time each day to focus on the present moment, and to be mindful of your thoughts and feelings. This can help you to be more aware of the good things in your life, and to appreciate the little moments that often go unnoticed.

Express gratitude:

Expressing gratitude to others is a powerful way to connect with this positive emotion. This can be as simple as writing a thank-you note, expressing your gratitude in person, or just sending positive thoughts to someone who has made a positive impact in your life.

Keep a gratitude journal:

Keeping a gratitude journal is a great way to reflect on the things you are thankful for each day. Write down three things you are grateful for each day, and look back on your journal regularly to see how your appreciation has grown over time.

Incorporate gratitude into your daily routines:

Take time to appreciate the little things in life, such as a beautiful sunset, a warm cup of tea, or a kind word from a friend. By incorporating gratitude into your daily routines, you will be able to connect with this positive emotion more easily.

Focus on the positive:

When faced with challenges or setbacks, focus on the positive aspects of your life. This can help you to maintain a positive outlook, and to be more resilient in the face of adversity.

Surround yourself with positive people:

Surrounding yourself with people who have a positive outlook on life can help you to maintain your own positive outlook. Seek out friends and family members who are supportive, and who encourage you to focus on the good things in your life.

By incorporating these strategies into your daily life, you can connect with gratitude and appreciation in a meaningful way, and experience the many benefits of this positive mindset. So, start today, and start living your best life!

"The more we appreciate the little things in life, the more we will be able to recognize and savor the big moments."

ꟿ

III

Creating a Positive Mindset with Gratitude and Appreciation

Gratitude and appreciation are powerful tools for creating a positive mindset. A positive mindset can help us to be more resilient in the face of challenges, to be happier, and to lead a more fulfilling life. In this chapter, we will explore how gratitude and appreciation can be used to create a positive mindset.

Recognize the power of your thoughts: Your thoughts have a powerful impact on your mood and outlook. By focusing on positive thoughts, you can create a positive mindset, and experience the benefits of gratitude and appreciation.

Practice gratitude daily:

Make gratitude a part of your daily routine. Take time each day to reflect on the things you are grateful for, and to express your gratitude to others. This will help you to develop a habit of gratitude, and to create a positive mindset.

Surround yourself with positive influences:

Seek out people, activities, and media that have a positive impact on your life. By surrounding yourself with positive influences, you will be more likely to maintain a positive outlook, even when faced with challenges.

Focus on the good:

When faced with negative thoughts or challenges, focus on the good things in your life. This can help you to maintain a positive outlook, and to be more resilient in the face of adversity.

Practice mindfulness:

Mindfulness can help you to be more aware of your thoughts and emotions, and to be more in control of them. By practicing mindfulness, you can create a positive mindset, and experience the benefits of gratitude and appreciation.

Set positive goals:

Setting positive goals for yourself can help you to maintain a positive mindset. Focus on goals that align with your values, and that will help you to lead a happier, more fulfilling life.

Celebrate your successes:

Celebrate your successes, no matter how small they may be. This can help you to maintain a positive outlook, and to be more resilient in the face of challenges.

By incorporating these strategies into your life, you can create a positive mindset with gratitude and appreciation. A positive mindset can help you to lead a happier, more fulfilling life, and to be more resilient in the face of challenges. So, start today, and create the positive mindset that you deserve!

"Living with gratitude means recognizing the beauty in the everyday and being thankful for it."

ନ୍ଦ

IV

Reframing Perspectives with Gratitude and Appreciation

Gratitude and appreciation are two of the most powerful tools we have to create a life of joy and contentment. When we take the time to recognize and appreciate the good in our lives, we can begin to shift our perspectives and open ourselves up to new possibilities.

Reframing our perspectives with gratitude and appreciation can help us to see the world in a different light. Instead of focusing on the negative, we can choose to focus on the positive. We can choose to be thankful for the blessings in our lives, no matter how small they may seem.

When we take the time to appreciate the good in our lives,

we can begin to see the world in a more positive light. We can start to recognize the beauty in the everyday moments and find joy in the small things. We can also start to recognize the good in others and be more open to giving and receiving love.

Reframing our perspectives with gratitude and appreciation can also help us to become more mindful and present in our lives. We can start to recognize the beauty in the present moment and be more aware of our thoughts and feelings. We can also start to recognize the interconnectedness of all things and be more open to the idea of living in harmony with the world around us.

"When we practice gratitude, we open ourselves up to a world of abundance and joy."

ꕥ

V

Practicing Mindful Gratitude and Appreciation"

Introduction:

Gratitude and appreciation are powerful emotions that can transform our lives, but they require regular practice to become a habit. In this chapter, we'll explore mindful practices that can help you cultivate an attitude of gratitude and appreciation.

Keeping a gratitude journal:

Start each day by writing down three things you're grateful for. This practice helps you focus on the positive and cultivate a habit of gratitude. Over time, you'll start to see patterns and realize how much you have to be thankful for.

Expressing gratitude:

Take time each day to express your gratitude to someone. It could be a simple thank you note, a phone call, or an in-person conversation. Regularly expressing gratitude strengthens relationships and helps us feel connected to others.

Mindful meditation:

Take time each day to practice mindfulness meditation. Focus on your breath and bring your attention to the present moment. While meditating, imagine yourself surrounded by everything you're grateful for. This practice can help you develop a more positive outlook on life.

Reframing challenges:

When faced with challenges, try to reframe them as opportunities for growth and learning. Instead of focusing on the negative, focus on what you can learn from the experience and what you can be grateful for. This shift in perspective can help you develop a more resilient mindset.

Engaging in acts of kindness:

Do something kind for someone else each day. This could be as simple as holding the door open for someone, or as complex as volunteering your time. Engaging in acts of kindness helps you feel connected to others and develops a sense of gratitude for all the good in your life.

Practicing gratitude and appreciation takes time and effort, but the benefits are well worth it. Incorporating these mindfulness practices into your daily routine can help you cultivate a more positive outlook on life, strengthen relationships, and develop a sense of gratitude for all the good in your life. Remember, gratitude and appreciation are habits that are developed over time, so be patient with yourself and stick with it. The more you practice, the easier it becomes and the more you'll be able to see the beauty and abundance in your life.

"Gratitude is a choice; it is a conscious decision to focus on the positive and be thankful for it."

ꙮ

VI

Cultivating Gratitude and Appreciation with Small Acts of Kindness

Introduction:

Gratitude and appreciation are powerful emotions that can transform our lives, but they often require a shift in perspective. In this chapter, we'll explore how small acts of kindness can help us cultivate gratitude and appreciation in our daily lives.

Showing appreciation to others:

Take time each day to show appreciation to those around you. Write a thank-you note, give someone a compliment, or simply offer a listening ear. By focusing on the positive qualities in others, you'll start to see the good in yourself and the world.

Giving to others:

Engage in acts of kindness, such as volunteering, donating to charity, or simply doing something thoughtful for a friend. When we give to others, we feel a sense of purpose and fulfillment that can cultivate gratitude and appreciation.

Practicing empathy:

Put yourself in others' shoes and try to understand their experiences. By understanding others, we develop a deeper appreciation for their perspectives and experiences. This can help us feel more connected to others and grateful for the relationships in our lives.

Engaging in acts of service:

Find ways to serve others, such as cooking a meal for a neighbor, helping someone with a task, or simply being there for someone in need. Engaging in acts of service helps us see the good in others and develops gratitude for the positive qualities in those around us.

Practicing gratitude:

Make gratitude a daily practice by writing down three things you're thankful for each day, expressing appreciation to those around you, or simply taking time to reflect on all the good in your life. Regularly practicing gratitude helps us see the world in a more positive light and develop an attitude of appreciation.

Small acts of kindness can have a big impact on our lives. By focusing on the good in others and giving to those around us, we can cultivate gratitude and appreciation in our daily lives. Remember, it's the little things that make a big difference, so start today by showing appreciation to someone and watch as the positive energy spreads. With time and practice, you'll find that gratitude and appreciation become a natural part of your daily routine, transforming the way you see the world and the people in it.

"The secret to living with gratitude is to be mindful of the present moment and all that it has to offer."

ᘛᘚ

VII

Celebrating Life's Victories with Gratitude and Appreciation

Introduction:

Gratitude and appreciation are often linked with positive experiences and accomplishments. In this chapter, we'll explore the power of celebrating life's victories with gratitude and appreciation.

Acknowledging accomplishments:

Take time to reflect on your accomplishments and acknowledge your hard work and dedication. This could mean writing down your achievements or simply taking a moment to be proud of yourself. By recognizing your own successes, you'll develop a sense of pride and gratitude for all you've achieved.

Celebrating with others:

Sharing your victories with friends and family can bring a sense of joy and fulfillment. Celebrating with others allows us to connect with those we love and develop gratitude for the relationships in our lives.

Gratitude for opportunities:

Be thankful for the opportunities life presents. Whether it's a new job, a trip, or a personal accomplishment, take a moment to appreciate the chance to grow and experience something new.

Appreciating the journey:

Remember to appreciate the journey, not just the destination. Take time to reflect on the challenges and growth that came with each victory. This will help you develop gratitude for the experiences and opportunities life provides.

Giving back:

Sharing your victories with others by giving back can be a powerful way to cultivate gratitude and appreciation. This could mean volunteering, donating to charity, or simply helping someone in need. By giving back, we show gratitude for the blessings in our lives and connect with those around us.

Celebrating life's victories with gratitude and appreciation can bring a sense of joy and fulfillment to our lives. By acknowledging our accomplishments, sharing our victories with others, and giving back, we can cultivate a positive attitude and transform our experiences. So next time you achieve a victory, take a moment to reflect on all you've accomplished and be grateful for the opportunities and growth that came with it. Remember, it's not just about the destination, but the journey and all the experiences along the way.

"Gratitude is a powerful emotion that can transform our lives and bring us closer to our true purpose."

VIII

Forgiving and Moving On with Gratitude and Appreciation

Introduction:

Forgiveness is a powerful tool that can help us move forward in life with a positive attitude. In this chapter, we'll explore how gratitude and appreciation can support the process of forgiving and moving on.

Understanding the power of forgiveness:

Forgiveness is a process that can help us let go of anger, resentment, and hurt. By forgiving, we free ourselves from negative emotions and gain the power to move forward in life.

Gratitude for personal growth:

Going through the process of forgiveness can bring a sense of gratitude for personal growth and understanding. Appreciating the growth that comes from challenging experiences can help us cultivate gratitude for the journey of life.

Appreciating the present moment:

Forgiveness allows us to focus on the present moment and appreciate the good things in our lives. It can help us to see the world through a lens of gratitude and develop a positive outlook on life.

Letting go of the past:

Forgiving and moving on can also help us let go of the past and focus on the present moment. By releasing past grudges and resentment, we free ourselves to experience joy, gratitude, and appreciation in the here and now.

Embracing a growth mindset:

Forgiveness can also help us embrace a growth mindset, seeing experiences as opportunities to grow and learn. By viewing challenges as opportunities, we can cultivate gratitude for the lessons and growth that come with them.

Forgiving and moving on with gratitude and appreciation can be a powerful way to transform negative experiences into positive ones. By understanding the power of forgiveness, embracing a growth mindset, and focusing on the present moment, we can cultivate a positive attitude and live with gratitude and appreciation every day. So next time you're facing a challenge or difficult situation, take a moment to reflect on the power of forgiveness and the growth that comes with it. Remember, by letting go of the past and embracing the present moment, we can find joy and gratitude in life.

"When we cultivate an attitude of appreciation, we open ourselves up to a world of possibility and joy."

ꟾ

IX

Appreciating Life's Little Moments of Joy

In our fast-paced and often stressful world, it can be easy to overlook the small moments of joy that bring us happiness. However, appreciating these little moments is essential for cultivating an attitude of gratitude and appreciation. In this chapter, we will explore the importance of appreciating life's little moments of joy and provide practical tips for doing so.

Pay attention to the present moment:

By focusing on the present moment, you can increase your awareness of the joyous moments that surround you. Take time to enjoy the beauty of nature, savor a delicious meal, or simply pause to appreciate the people in your life.

Find joy in everyday activities:

From cooking a meal to taking a walk, everyday activities can bring us joy if we take the time to appreciate them. Try to find joy in the simple things in life, such as listening to music, reading a book, or watching a movie.

Celebrate small victories:

Whether it's completing a task at work or simply making it through a difficult day, take time to celebrate your successes, no matter how small. This can boost your confidence and help you to appreciate the progress you've made.

Practice gratitude:

Take time each day to reflect on the things you are grateful for, both big and small. This will help you to cultivate an attitude of gratitude and appreciation for the little moments of joy in your life.

Connect with loved ones:

Spending time with loved ones can bring us happiness and help us to appreciate the little moments of joy in our lives. Whether it's going out for a meal, sharing a hobby, or simply spending time together, connecting with loved ones can bring us joy and a sense of gratitude.

Find the humor in life:

Humor is a great way to appreciate the little moments of joy in life. Try to find the humor in difficult situations and don't take life too seriously.

Give back:

Giving back to others, whether it's through volunteering, donating to charity, or simply helping a neighbor, can bring us joy and help us to appreciate the little moments of happiness in our lives.

By taking the time to appreciate life's little moments of joy, you can cultivate an attitude of gratitude and appreciation. This can help you to lead a happier, more fulfilling life and increase your resilience in the face of adversity. So, start today and appreciate the little moments of joy in your life!

"Living with gratitude means recognizing the beauty in the small moments and being thankful for them."

ꙮ

X

Choosing a Path of Gratitude and Appreciation

Introduction:

In this chapter, we will explore the importance of choosing a path of gratitude and appreciation. By making this choice, we can cultivate a positive attitude and live a life filled with joy and satisfaction.

Understanding the power of choice:

One of the most powerful things we can do in life is to choose our thoughts and attitudes. By choosing to focus on gratitude and appreciation, we can create a positive outlook and live a life filled with joy and fulfillment.

The impact of gratitude on our lives:

Gratitude and appreciation have been shown to have a positive impact on our physical and emotional health, relationships, and overall well-being. By making the choice to cultivate gratitude and appreciation, we can improve all areas of our lives.

Gratitude as a habit:

By making gratitude and appreciation a habit, we can create a positive cycle of joy and satisfaction. The more we focus on what we are grateful for, the more we find to be grateful for. This creates a virtuous cycle that can bring happiness and fulfillment to every aspect of our lives.

The role of mindfulness in gratitude:

Mindfulness can be a powerful tool in choosing a path of gratitude and appreciation. By being present in the moment and fully engaged with our experiences, we can cultivate a deep appreciation for life and all it has to offer.

Overcoming obstacles:

Choosing a path of gratitude and appreciation is not always easy, and we may face obstacles along the way. However, by being mindful and intentional in our focus, we can overcome these challenges and continue to cultivate a positive attitude and live with gratitude and appreciation.

By choosing a path of gratitude and appreciation, we can transform our lives and live with joy and fulfillment. By making gratitude a habit and being mindful of our thoughts and experiences, we can create a positive cycle of joy and satisfaction. So make the choice today to focus on gratitude and appreciation and start living a life filled with joy and happiness.

"The secret to living with gratitude is to be mindful of the blessings in our lives and express our appreciation for them."

XI

Finding Inspiration in Nature with Gratitude and Appreciation

Introduction:

Nature has a way of inspiring us and bringing us peace and tranquility. In this chapter, we will explore the connection between gratitude, appreciation, and nature and how it can help us cultivate a positive outlook on life.

The beauty of nature:

Nature is a source of beauty and wonder, and it has the power to captivate us with its majesty and grandeur. By taking the time to appreciate the beauty of nature, we can cultivate gratitude and appreciation for the world around us.

The benefits of being in nature:

Studies have shown that spending time in nature has numerous benefits for our physical and mental health. By connecting with nature, we can reduce stress, improve mood, and boost overall well-being.

Finding inspiration in nature:

Nature has a way of inspiring us and reminding us of the simple things in life. By taking time to slow down and fully engage with our natural surroundings, we can find inspiration and a sense of peace.

Gratitude walks:

One way to connect with nature and cultivate gratitude is to take a gratitude walk. This involves taking a leisurely stroll in a natural setting and focusing on the things we are grateful for. This can help us cultivate gratitude and appreciation for the world around us.

Nature journaling:

Nature journaling is another way to connect with nature and cultivate gratitude. This involves taking time to reflect on our experiences in nature and writing down what we are grateful for. This can be a powerful tool for cultivating gratitude and appreciation.

Nature has the power to inspire us and bring us peace and

tranquility. By taking the time to connect with nature and cultivate gratitude, we can live with a positive outlook and appreciation for the world around us. So make the choice today to explore the beauty of nature and start finding inspiration and joy in the world around you.

"Gratitude is a powerful force that can bring us closer to our true potential and help us live a life of joy and contentment."

ꕥ

XII

Understanding the Power of Gratitude and Appreciation in Difficult Times

Introduction:

Life can be challenging at times, but it's during these difficult moments that gratitude and appreciation can play a crucial role in helping us to maintain a positive outlook and find meaning in our experiences. In this chapter, we'll explore the power of gratitude and appreciation during difficult times.

Gratitude as a coping mechanism:

Gratitude has been shown to be an effective coping mechanism during difficult times. By focusing on what we are grateful for, we can shift our attention away from negative thoughts and feelings, reducing stress and anxiety.

The role of appreciation in difficult times:

Appreciation has a similar impact during difficult times. By focusing on what we appreciate in our lives, we can find meaning and purpose, even during the toughest of circumstances.

Gratitude journaling:

Gratitude journaling is a powerful tool for cultivating gratitude and appreciation during difficult times. By taking time each day to write down what we are grateful for, we can shift our focus from negative thoughts and feelings to positive ones.

Finding gratitude in the present moment:

One of the keys to cultivating gratitude and appreciation during difficult times is to focus on the present moment. By focusing on what we are grateful for in the moment, we can find peace and solace, even during the toughest of circumstances.

The power of community:

The support of loved ones and our community can play a crucial role in helping us to cultivate gratitude and appreciation during difficult times. By connecting with others and sharing our experiences, we can find comfort and support, helping us to maintain a positive outlook.

Difficult times are a part of life, but they don't have to be overwhelming. By cultivating gratitude and appreciation, we can maintain a positive outlook, find meaning and purpose, and weather the storms of life with grace and resilience. So, when you're facing tough times, turn to the power of gratitude and appreciation and find peace and hope in even the most difficult of circumstances.

"When we practice gratitude, we open ourselves up to a world of abundance and fulfillment."

ꟹ

XIII

Connecting to Inner Peace with Gratitude and Appreciation

Introduction:

Inner peace is a state of mind that allows us to experience calm, contentment, and fulfillment, even in the midst of chaos and turmoil. In this chapter, we'll explore the relationship between gratitude, appreciation, and inner peace.

The relationship between gratitude and inner peace:

Gratitude has been shown to have a powerful impact on our sense of inner peace. By focusing on what we are grateful for, we can shift our focus away from negative thoughts and feelings, allowing us to experience calm and serenity.

The role of appreciation in connecting to inner peace:

Appreciation also plays an important role in connecting to inner peace. By focusing on what we appreciate in our lives, we can find meaning and purpose, even during the busiest and most hectic of times.

Mindfulness and gratitude:

Mindfulness and gratitude go hand in hand in connecting to inner peace. By practicing mindfulness and focusing on what we are grateful for, we can quiet our minds, reduce stress, and find inner peace.

The power of positive affirmations:

Positive affirmations can also help us connect to inner peace. By repeating affirmations that focus on gratitude and appreciation, we can shift our focus away from negative thoughts and feelings, allowing us to experience calm and serenity.

Cultivating gratitude and appreciation in daily life:

Incorporating gratitude and appreciation into our daily lives is key to connecting to inner peace. Whether through gratitude journaling, mindfulness practices, or simply taking time each day to reflect on what we are grateful for, we can find inner peace, even in the midst of chaos.

Inner peace is a state of mind that allows us to experience

calm, contentment, and fulfillment, even in the midst of chaos and turmoil. By cultivating gratitude and appreciation, we can connect to inner peace, reducing stress and anxiety, and finding meaning and purpose in our lives. So, turn to the power of gratitude and appreciation, and experience the peace and serenity that come from connecting to your inner self.

"The key to living with gratitude is to be mindful of the present moment and all that it has to offer, and to express our appreciation for it."

ଌ

XIV

Discovering the Abundance of Gratitude and Appreciation in Life

Introduction:

Gratitude and appreciation have the power to change our lives in profound and meaningful ways. In this chapter, we'll explore how gratitude and appreciation can help us discover the abundance in our lives and live a more fulfilling life.

The power of gratitude and appreciation to shift our perspectives:

By focusing on what we are grateful for and what we appreciate in our lives, we can shift our perspectives from a scarcity mentality to an abundance mentality. This shift can help us see the world in a more positive light and experience a greater sense of abundance in our lives.

The impact of gratitude and appreciation on our relationships:

Gratitude and appreciation can also help us strengthen our relationships. By expressing gratitude and appreciation for those around us, we can build deeper and more meaningful connections with others.

How gratitude and appreciation can lead to greater success:

Gratitude and appreciation can also lead to greater success in our careers and personal lives. By focusing on what we are grateful for, we can increase our motivation, productivity, and overall satisfaction in our lives.

The impact of gratitude and appreciation on our mental and physical health: Expressing gratitude and appreciation has been shown to have a positive impact on our mental and physical health. By focusing on what we are grateful for, we can reduce stress, improve our mood, and even boost our immune system.

How gratitude and appreciation can help us live in the present moment: Gratitude and appreciation can also help us live in the present moment, allowing us to fully experience and enjoy the present, rather than dwelling on the past or worrying about the future.

Gratitude and appreciation have the power to change our lives in profound and meaningful ways. By focusing on what we are grateful for and what we appreciate in our lives, we can shift our perspectives, strengthen our relationships, experience greater success, and improve our mental and physical health. So, embrace the power of gratitude and appreciation, and discover the abundance in your life.

"Cultivating an attitude of appreciation is the secret to unlocking a life of joy and fulfillment."

ꕥ

XV

Understanding the Benefits of Gratitude and Appreciation

Gratitude and appreciation are powerful emotions that have a profound impact on our lives. From improving our mental and physical health to enhancing our relationships and overall well-being, the benefits of gratitude and appreciation are numerous and wide-ranging. In this chapter, we will explore the various benefits of gratitude and appreciation and why it is essential to cultivate these emotions in our daily lives.

Improved mental health:

Gratitude and appreciation have been shown to reduce stress, anxiety, and depression, and improve our overall well-being. By focusing on the positive aspects of our lives and appreciating what we have, we can reduce feelings of negativity and increase our happiness.

Stronger relationships:

Gratitude and appreciation can enhance our relationships by strengthening bonds and fostering positive communication. By showing appreciation for others, we can increase their happiness and foster a sense of connection and intimacy in our relationships.

Physical health benefits:

Gratitude and appreciation have been linked to numerous physical health benefits, including improved sleep, reduced inflammation, and a stronger immune system. By appreciating what we have, we can improve our overall health and well-being.

Increased resilience:

Gratitude and appreciation can help us to build resilience and bounce back from setbacks and challenges. By focusing on what we are grateful for, we can develop a positive outlook on life and increase our ability to overcome adversity.

Better decision making:

Gratitude and appreciation can improve our decision-making skills by helping us to focus on what is important and prioritize our values. By appreciating the present moment and our experiences, we can make decisions that are aligned with our goals and priorities.

Increased creativity:

Gratitude and appreciation have been linked to increased creativity, as they help us to see the world in a new and more positive light. By focusing on what we are grateful for, we can open ourselves up to new possibilities and explore new avenues for creative expression.

More fulfilling life:

Gratitude and appreciation can help us to lead a more fulfilling life by increasing our overall happiness and well-being. By taking the time to appreciate what we have and the people in our lives, we can create a sense of meaning and purpose that is essential for a fulfilling life.

Gratitude and appreciation are powerful emotions that have numerous benefits for our mental and physical health, relationships, and overall well-being. By cultivating an attitude of gratitude and appreciation, we can lead a happier, more fulfilling life and improve our resilience in the face of adversity. So, start today and embrace the power of gratitude and appreciation!

"Gratitude is a choice; it is an intentional act of recognizing the positive and expressing appreciation. By making the conscious decision to be thankful, we can cultivate a mindset of abundance and joy."

☙

Other Books Of The Author

1. The Moments When I Met God
2. Kashiyile Theertha Pathangal
3. GURU GYAN VANI
4. Abhiprerak Gita
5. ASSI SE JAIN GHAT TAK
6. Hopelessness of Arjuna
7. The Soul and It's True Nature
8. Sense of Action (Karma)
9. Action through Wisdom
10. Action through Wisdom
11. THEORY AND PRACTICAL OF EVERY ACTION
12. LOGICAL UNDERSTANDING OF THE SUPREME
13. THE IMPERISHABLE SUPREME
14. Yatra Nishadraj se Hanuman Ghat Tak
15. Yatra Karnatak Ghat se Raja Ghat Tak
16. Yatra Pandey Ghat se Prayagraj Ghat Tak
17. Yatra Ranjendra Prasad Ghat se Dattatreya Ghat Tak
18. YaatraSindhiya Ghat se Gwaliar Ghat Tak
19. Yatra Mangala Gauri Ghat se Hanuman Gadhi Ghat Tak
20. Yatra Gaay Ghat Se Nishad Ghat Tak
21. MAA GANGA, GHATEN EVM UTSAV
22. Ganga Arti Dev Deepavali evam Any Utsav
23. Potentials of Digitalized India
24. VEDIC CONSCIOUSNESS
25. A Brief Introduction to Vedic Science
26. Kashi ke Barah Jyotirling
27. IMPACT OF MOTIVATION
28. Let's have a Milky Way Journey
29. Color Therapy in a Nutshell

30. Rigveda in a Nutshell
31. Yajurveda in a Nutshell
32. Samveda in a Nutshell
33. Atharva Veda in a Nutshell
34. Ayushman Bhava - Ayurveda
35. Srimad Bhagavad Gita and Upanishad Connection
36. Srimad Bhagavad Gita - an attempt to summarize each chapter.
37. Facts and Impact of Nakshatra
38. Astro Gems - NAVARATNA
39. Ekadashi - A Concise Overview
40. A Concise View of Hanuman Chalisa
41. Inspirational Gita
42. Nakshatraranyam
43. Summary of 18 Mahapuranas
44. Synopsis of 18 Upa Puranas
45. Rigvediya Upanishads
46. Shukla Yajurvediya Upanishads
47. Krishna Yajurvediya Upanishads
48. Samavediya Upanishads
49. Atharvavediya Upanishads
50. The Seven Great Sages
51. From Rocket Scientist to President Dr. APJ Abdul Kalam
52. The Visionary's Voice - Quotes of Dr. APJ Abdul Kalam
53. The Wisdom of Swami Vivekananda: Insights and Inspiration from a Legendary Spiritual Teacher
54. Ayurvedic Remedies from the Garden
55. Sages and Seers
56. Rising Strong – Motivational Stories of Women
57. Beyond Flames -Mystery stories of Funeral Ghat Manikarnika
58. The Origins of Tulsi: A Look at the Mythological Roots of the Plant"

59. The Holistic Cow: A Look at the Physical, Spiritual, and Cultural Importance of Cows in India
60. Arts of Healing
61. Exploring the Divine
62. Understanding Five Elements
63. The Etymology of Ram
64. Symbols of India
65. Voice of Change (About Speeches of Great Men)
66. She Speaks (About Speeches of Great Women)
67. Patriotism on Celluloid – Brief About Patriotic Films
68. The Music of Motivation: A Brief Guide to Inspirational Film Songs
69. **Unlocking the Secrets of the Dashopanishads**
70. A Cultural Mosaic
71. Ancient Traditions, Modern Minds
72. Ecos of Ancient Wisdom
73. Beneath the Surface
74. From Temples to Ashrams
75. Sages of the Subcontinent
76. The Art of Healling (Ayurveda, Yoga & Naturopathy)
77. Indian Kitchen
78. The Festivals of India
79. The Indian Epics Retold
80. The Power of Mantras
81. The Indian River Ganges
82. The Indian Architecture
83. Rites of Passage
84. The Indian Silk Road
85. The Indian Literature
86. The Indian Villages
87. The Indian Folks & Crafts
88. The Way of Buddha
89. The Ramayan of Tulsidas

90. Astrological Remedies
91. The Secret Power of Motivation
92. Secret of Developing your Inner Strength
93. The Secret Path to Motivation
94. The Art and Secret of Positive Thinking
95. The Secrets of Practicing Ethical Living
96. Indian Art and Painting
97. The Indian Herbalism
98. Bharatanatyam to Kathak
99. Exploring India's Astrological Remedies
100. The Indian Festival of Flowers
101. Indian Handicrafts
102. The Splashes of Joy – India's Colour Festival
103. The Indian Science of Astrology
104. The Indian Mythology
105. Path to Enlightenment
106. The Indian Spirituality for Children
107. Aromas of India
108. The Secrets of Healthy Relationships
109. Ancestral Ties
110. The Indian Street Food
111. Discovering America
112. The Indian Textile
113. Listening to Motivational Speeches
114. Taste of India
115. A Cultural Journey through Indian Nuptials
116. Motivational Quote for Change
117. Secret Strategies for Making Money
118. Secrets to Cultivate a Positive Mindset
119. A Tapestry of Cultures: Exploring India from Kashmir to Kanyakumari
120. Achieving Your Dreams with Resilience: Secret Strategies for Overcoming Obstacles

121. Innovative Startups - 25 Startup Ideas to Spark Your Business Creativity
122. Export Management: Strategies for Global Success
123. Exporting from India - A Step by Step Guide
124. Finance Fundamentals: Mastering Financial Management for Business Success
125. Global Growth Strategies for International Business Development
126. Marketing Mastery: Unlocking the Secrets of Modern Marketing
127. Operations Mastery: Managing the Flow of Value in Business
128. Strategic Business Management: Navigating the Modern Business Landscape
129. Human Resource Management Strategies for Building and Managing a High Performance Team
130. The Indian Landscapes and Nature: An Exploration Of India's Natural Beauty And Diversity
131. The Indian Street Performances: A Cultural Exploration of India's Street Performances
132. Affirming Your Self-Worth: Strategies for Achieving Emotional Wellbeing
133. Cultivating Self-Discipline: Secrets Methods for Achieving Your Goals
134. Embracing Change: Strategies for Adapting to Life's Challenges
135. Embracing Your Uniqueness: Secret Strategies for Living an Authentic Life
136. Finding Motivation in Despondency: Coping with Difficult Times
137. Embracing Change
138. Learning to Love Yourself
139. Managing Time for Yourself

140. Unlock the keys to Self-Motivation
141. Secret to Boost Confidence
142. Unlocking your Potential: A Path to Innerstrengh & Success
143. Secrets to Develop Authentic Relationship

Contact

DR. JAGADEESH PILLAI

MBA & PhD in Vedic Science

Four Times Guinness World Record Holder

Winner of Mahatma Gandhi Vishwa Shanti Puraskar and
Global Peace Ambassador

Gemology, Astro & Vastu Consultant - Spiritual Counselor

Consultant for designing World Record Ideas

Efficient Tarot Card Reader

9839093003

myrichindia@gmail.com

drjagadeeshpillai@facebook

drjagadeeshpillai@instagram
jagadeeshpillai@youtube

www. JAGADEESHPILLAI.com

|| LOKAHA SAMASTHAHA SUKHINO BHAVANTU ||

ജ

9 798889 593225

Printed by Libri Plureos GmbH in Hamburg, Germany